POLITE OCCASIONS

By

Anne Babson

Published by Unsolicited Press

www.unsolicitedpress.com

Copyright © 2018 Anne Babson

All Rights Reserved.

Unsolicited Press Books are distributed to the trade by Ingram.

ISBN: 978-1-947021-30-3

Cover design: UP Team

Font: Adobe Caslon Pro

"So then because thou art lukewarm, and neither cold nor hot, I will spew thee out of my mouth."

— Revelation 3:16

"Be careful not to let amiable discussion turn into contradiction and argument."

— Emily Post

To LW

TABLE OF CONTENTS

THE FIRST SEAL	1
YOUR FIRST POEM	3
THE RECOUNTING OF A POLITE OCCASION	6
WELCOME WAGON	9
HOW TO	11
TRIBULATION LYRIC #1	13
THINGS I SHOULD HAVE DONE BY NOW	14
BETWEEN THE KEYS	16
THE VICTORIOUS CHRISTIAN COUPLE	17
WEDDING DISHES	19
LOOKING FOR YOU IN THE SINK OF DISHES	21
TRIBULATION LYRIC #7	22
WHILE YOU WERE OUT	23
TRIBULATION LYRIC #4	24
THE SECOND SEAL	25
THE WALL SPEAKS	26
PALMISTRY	28
PATMOS LYRIC 3	30
AT THAT TIME IN THE CITY	31
AFTER THE GREAT SPEECH	37
PATMOS LYRIC #4	39

ABOUT THE MUD	40
THE AGING BOND GIRL CALLS HER BEST FRIEND	41
THE ASTRONAUT'S WIFE	44
THE SHARK AND THE BODYGUARD	46
MICROSOFT COMPANY PORTRAIT 1978 -- AND PROPHECY	49
PATMOS LYRIC #2	55
PATMOS LYRIC #1	56
THE THIRD SEAL	57
THE METHOD	58
WHAT I AM NOT WRITING	60
TRIBULATION LYRIC #3	63
THE CENTER	64
THE UNBORN	66
THE FOURTH SEAL	99
SCREEN PLAY	100
DECEIT OF MUSICALS	104
BOTTICELLI AFTER SAVANAROLA	106
LINER NOTES	108
CONCERT	111
THE END OF SINGING	113

SUBTERRANEAN LYRIC #1	115
SNAILS	117
SUNBURN CUISINE	119
THE DRUNKEN MONORAIL	121
SKIING IN IRAN	122
PILGRIM LYRIC	124
Acknowledgements	126
About the Author	128

THE FIRST SEAL

"And he causeth all…to receive a mark in their right hand, or in their foreheads: And that no man might buy or sell, save he that had the mark, or the name of the beast, or the number of his name. Here is wisdom."

— Revelation 13:16-18

'The visiting card has entirely taken the place of the written note of invitation to informal parties of every description. Messages of condolence or congratulation are written on it."

— Emily Post

YOUR FIRST POEM

Generals know children, inspired by battle hymns,
Walk through mine fields. I write in a gunmetal tower.
I never meet the Generals. But now I meet
You, first name inspired by a flower, and you hand
       It to me, saying, "This is my first poem."

Your cheek throbs, feet tap cotillions. I tell you
Niceties told for centuries, so droningly
They hypnotize the angels who do not know why
They salivate at the bell. The first time you have heard
These words, you respond spontaneously, no slave
       To Pavlov: "This is my first poem."

Generals keep deadlines. Rent falls due on the first,

The fifteenth -- other bills. The children need new slogans.
They hear the old ones too often, suspect the worst.
But still you stand here, messy-headed, giggle-prone,
Uncowed, while God Himself --
       Himself -- Surely this world

Is a male's invention -- repeats the ice floes, the
Mud slides, and the scurrying of insects, but
      Out of season, you say: "This is my first poem."

You ask me to read it, a first-time-reading read.
My gunmetal desk gets stacked with manuals, not
Villanelles. The sharpener works on pencils, not
Wits. But your blossoms buzz, and Generals, their
Faces veiled by chrome and concrete, must be benign.
You have written a thing. It belongs to you. You
Offer it like a hymen to me, as I write
Generals' battle hymns, weighing me, on your scales,
Heavily. You humble me before bleary-eyed
God Himself and the undead angels, who, as I
Write these blasted battle hymns, turning phrase
      Into phrase into end-rhyme, child into soldier
      Into hamburger scattered, spin constellations,
Turning Spring into Summer into me into
      Another butler for the Generals. You
      Humble me, praying,
The first-time prayer gets prayed, "This is my first poem."

A General's undersecretary buzzes.
      I pick up, then pick up, then scurry. You ask
           Again, and waiting for the elevator down,
                I wonder how to tell you the original
Is you, the atoms split by battle are forged, the

Generals are ghouls, the children are my lampshades.
My last original thought blew out when I braved
The windy tunnel of this gunmetal tower.
The dogs in Heaven salivate, the bell chimes, the
Zombies open the pearly gates, not invading
But escaping. The only one left is you.
           This is your first poem?

        Hide it in a safe place.

THE RECOUNTING OF A POLITE OCCASION

An absinthe-soaked sugar cube of well-planned nonchalance festers in my throat, infects it with unspeakable secrets. I should shudder, but instead, I shrug. My chords scrape hoarse from *"Thank you!"* to party crashers who don't deserve it -- especially from crooning it to you. Fatally polite, I wait for my kindness to kill my enemies in this grand baroque tea house, in this cobweb-strewn parlor, but you don't seem at all close to dying from it. Did you know that I swallow bitter pills now, four before every meal? They promise to help me lose, fit precisely into this itchy matron's tea-dance ball gown you bequeathed to me for this polite occasion.

I find no room for outrage in the cleavage of this gift dress, no room for cursing around the zipper up the hips -- only for, *"Please pass me"* the moldering watercress sandwiches, and for *"Would you care for some more"* of the urine-flavored tea. I find no room in the waistline for screaming or sharp laughter. You say I look nice. I somehow manage to wheeze out, *"I adore sitting here with you. My, what lovely weather we are having."*

I wish the sleeves held room for me to reach across the table and slap you back, that the collar sat less high and tight, that I might tell you how much I wish you would go home. I smile so gamely while it strangles me that you are too arrogant to suppose how much I loathe it, that your grandbaby at my sagging breast will leech me dry one sad day, that the successful husband who now nightly hammers at my hipbones will imagine that I am somebody else at that crucial moment -- the one where your litanies to a male God are answered, then roll over and snore. Watch how I caress his arm -- look how tenderly I gaze up at him while he speaks to you! "Are you having as much fun as we are?" He asks you, and you nod.

I used to wait for the day my grunting husband would love me savagely. I would wear a hide sarong on a tandoori-baked island, while I hunted wild hare, breaking necks in snares, roasting on a spit. Instead, I speak French fluently and know niceties from the official languages of the United Nations. No Crusoe, I, and you no Friday -- This apartment is no mud hut. I own three complete sets of European hand-painted china and two sets of wedding silver. Some of it is monogrammed with your initials. I regret hungrily I have neither killed an animal for food nor an in-law for sport, but, lest we forget, this is a polite occasion, one where nothing compels the crashers to leave.

I dread the pending day I sit sedated in some suburb, in a house with its own flagpole, an island in the kitchen, and a television in each room so that someone else never misses a game. I sense my own irrelevance welling up in my throat, waiting for the day I can howl it out -- in attic while an *au pair* takes the stroller through the petting zoo -- that should happen in about five years -- I can hardly wait for those next few minutes of personal time! Then I can finally rip this itchy thing off me for a deep breath before I gather it up again, go downstairs to serve the next meal, proffer to you a few excuses for my odd, momentary absence.

WELCOME WAGON

"Welcome,"
        The basket's ribbon curls, and I
        Understand the stretch of the arms holding
        It toward me.

"Welcome,
        But stay at arm's length.
        We know why you have come here. You Have fooled
        No one with your witness protection name."

"Welcome,
        You refugee from disaster unnamed,
        Not like many hurricanes named female,
        Not like many downstate divorces, named
        Man's last name versus man's last name."

"Welcome,
        But stand back.
        You've not fooled anyone with
        That chintz, those lawn chairs, those Perennials
        That die every fall. Your kind arrives here
        With every hard closing on a house sale.

"Welcome.

                We know you have barely survived what Chased
                You here. We smell the gunpowder in the
                Folds of your 'kiss the cook' apron."

                We were once you but won't admit it, not
                Even to ourselves in private."

"Welcome,

                But that past you brought with you onto the
                Cul de sac, like the wolf-sized dogs or
                Coal mine canaries the bylaws reject
                In this gated community, you had
                Better take it out, have it put to sleep."

HOW TO

1. When they look at you the way they look at you, don't look at them the way you look at them. No one will know the difference. Just look through them at whatever you wish you could see instead.

2. They may cry. When they hug you and tell you how sorry they are, pretend you don't want to spit. No one will know the difference. Lick your lips instead. Be careful not to bite them until they bleed.

3. They are frightened. Nothing you can say or do will calm them. Pretend that the tragedy was theirs, not yours. No one will know the difference, and this will prevent any lull in conversation.

4. None of them will guess you are angry with them. No one will know the difference. If possible, place them in pairs throughout the party so that they can congratulate each other.

5. Feeling humiliated can be a real plus. Stay at home and work on quilting projects. Learn a new language with downloads bought

online. Chat in language with strangers far away. Create a screen name that misleads them. Use someone else's photo in your profile. No one will know the difference.

6. There is no tip number 6. Try again.

7. Hostesses agree. The best policy is scorched earth. Serve blackened cat fish with our regret remoulade *(see recipe in index).*

8. Don't be surprised if they accuse you in the end. It's easier than admitting a theodicy. Offer them a spritzer of muddled mint and cheap bourbon. Don't expect gratitude.

9. They will soon find your woes insufficiently novel and move to the next house. Serve our Celtic black veil wassail to attract new carolers *(recipe listed under "tombstone accessories.")*

10. Remember that less is more. Less is also less. Less is loss. Loss is less. No one will know the difference. Hang mistletoe above the police barricade to make it romantic.

TRIBULATION LYRIC #1

After the explosions, I drove to the police
Station with a ribboned box packed with Italian
Sugar cookies. I smiled, handed them to an
Officer trying to keep his spine from curling
Into coils. He had not seen home in days. *"Here.*
For you." I had felt sorry for all of them.
They shoved me into the interrogation room.
They demanded proof. After chemical tests turned
Up no toxins, and whacking me with a sack of
Frozen oranges produced no oracle, they
Uncuffed me. Trembling right hand, I missed sticking the
Key in the ignition. I sat panting, then aimed
Again. The motor hiccupped, and then it hit me:
"Oh. This, too, is the aftershock."

THINGS I SHOULD HAVE DONE BY NOW

1. I should have taken your hand and rubbed spit into it to get your attention so that you might believe when I told you we share a destination.

2. I should have dug the hole, the one that leads there

3. I should have explained why reading this list produces an attack of stomach butterfly locusts

4. I should have gotten you to sign your name to the bottom of this, our Mayflower Compact.

5. I should have explained – you are a numbers person, not a person of letters – how these words were breadcrumbs for the others to follow us later.

6. I should have grabbed that hand of yours, which would have become a little sticky and ink-stained, and walked you to the very precipice.

7. I should have kissed you, not so much romantically as politically, the way two people on the same side of an important question do.

8. I should have held your face in my hands.

9. I should have let go and turned.

10. I should have jumped.

BETWEEN THE KEYS

On the piano there is a note -- listen – it is playing now.
It does not fit tidily onto the scale. It is a squawk.
It cannot be commanded but by plucking the strings
Inside with a decisive plunk. It is inconvenient to try
To reach it. Listen. Sometimes, though, when all the other
Notes are taking a nap, and nothing seems to quite fit
That hangs in one's closet, and the cat's gaze is following
An invisible piece of lint or the reflection of a watch,
And the dog, who normally follows one around the
House all day, has gone missing, tip-toe downstairs
And listen quietly. If the window is open, and the
Breeze catches the curtains, the Steinway may
Just belch out such a tone and seem to say
"Pardon me," by covering its long ivory teeth.

THE VICTORIOUS CHRISTIAN COUPLE

Hallelujah -- The victorious Christian couple
Attends church together, and after the last amen, strolls --
Can I get another amen -- where the leaves leap
Off branches, committing suicide – amen -- but they
Call this autumn, not a mass cult exodus, nothing to take
Personally. When they start talking at the same time, each says,
"No, you first," laughing delicately as the wind picks up.
They sigh at the gravel path, hold hands passionately, stowing
The rest for later: "Do not open until marriage" is written
On a gift tag stitched to the woman's brassiere of ribbon --
Selah -- And egg shell crepe paper with matching panties,
The man's white cotton boxers padlocked and alarmed.
They don't even call this a date until they have set a date.
Much remains unspoken, except in silent prayer. To forget,
They discuss everything else they can think of except "it."

> The members of the victorious Christian couple Worry
> less than the defeated couple making out on The park
> bench they pass -- those two have only Locked tongues
> to be sure that the other one doesn't Wander off

Again, are stroking each other on parts that would Hurt if somebody squeezed them hard and shouted, "You can't leave me yet! Not until I say so!" -- but Let's be honest – Amen -- Those two who do it to Snoop Dogg

Duets, with woofs and scratches, slaps And pap smears, their clothes don't smell as clean, But their jokes are funnier -- Glory be-- with more Pain in them. The ideas sound more original -- sin always seems like innovation

At first, until things end the same old way -- and if These couples left the park at the same moment – Amen -- the benched

Sinners might cross into incoming traffic for the Adrenaline rush of it.

WEDDING DISHES

Given to you in exchange for the breaking of
The saucer between your thighs, the set of bloodless
Blue silver-rimmed mirrors, salad-, bread- and dinner-
> Sized, enough for twelve. You stashed them
> Under tea towels in earthquake-proof canisters, Afraid of
> what the jury might do to them.
> You promised yourself their use for some grand
> Occasion, grander than your wedding, than births,
> Anniversaries, moveable feasts, raises,

Graduations, leave-takings. You never once set
Them out. Don't touch them, you warned me.
Those are for special days impervious to the
> Passing of the hours, the cycle, then cessation,
> The graying, drooping, wrinkling, liver-spotting.
> Then you got the news -- you were waning. Still you Left
> them under heavy wraps, cryogenically sealed
> For some future when you would not partake in the
> Breaking of bread. They sit now in my cabinet.

I inherited them all virginal, still uncrossed
By a single butter knife. I set them out like

Flat full moons every twenty-eight days. Though they
      Are the ice blue for which you registered, I heap
      On them my roasted red peppers, my scarlet
      Bruschetta, my berry sorbets, my purpling beets,
           My bloody meats, my ripe nectarines,
           My marinara and my moussaka. They have
           Finally entered the coursing stream of family,
A place where at last good things are fed to good people
Who waited so long to be invited to the table.

LOOKING FOR YOU IN THE SINK OF DISHES

I reach into water and grab the sponge.
My ink-stained fingers ungloved feel the grit.
I dredge for meaning in the moldering grunge
Of a sink as dirty as a glob of spit.

It is Proust's muffin that makes me plunge
Naked fingers into the muck of it.
I reach into water and grab the sponge.
My ink-stained fingers ungloved feel the grit.

Food triggers memory I would expunge.
I scrape with thumbs, not a steel wool mitt.
The soap promises polish that won't quit.
Elbow grease removes *ce que Proust mange*.
I reach into water and grab the sponge.

TRIBULATION LYRIC #7

At their house, the front door swung half open,
As if Missus Beekman had wandered out to
Clip some more of her roses, like she does,
Or did, but inside, nothing got burgled.
At the table: a half-eaten apple
A bowl of Corn Chex, a glass of grape juice.
The master bedroom shower still sprayed on,
Squirting the granite tiles, soap cap open,
A pair of Missus Beekman's underpants
laid out with some of her pantyhose,
one of her business suits, a red scarf
On the blue bedspread. The phone fell off the hook,
I guess. Normally, I clean for them, but the house smells
Of roses, roses I can't find, and no clippers.

WHILE YOU WERE OUT

I looked in corners where lint gathers.
I realized you had hidden everything.
I took the last load of laundry you left;
It felt lighter – a soulless corpse –
Than when I gathered its bundle before.

Your father shuffles when he walks.
He says little. Your name has become unutterable.
I go to church without him.
I took communion, took it again.
The body tastes just like bread.
That blood – you would swear it was grape juice,
Yet I seek transubstantiation, not
Just scraps from the last meal before
Easter weekend when everything ended.

TRIBULATION LYRIC #4

If you get this message, stranger, it means I'm gone.
I have left it in my wallet for you filled with cash.
I know you have meant to rob me, friend. Take it all.
This, however, is more valuable – this word.
Feel free to use my car keys as well. I have no
Heirs behind me. Just read
What I have put in this booklet. I hope
You can understand. Yeshuah turned to the thief
On his right and said, smiling, "This day shall you be
With me in Paradise." I turn to you. I have
No power to draw you up here with me, but know,
Thief, it is not quite too late for you, not quite, and
If you follow instructions in this manual,
You just might survive what's next long enough to see
Me smiling on something other than the driver's
License in this wallet. This day, this day He made good.

THE SECOND SEAL

"Standing afar off for the fear of her torment, saying, Alas, alas, that great city Babylon, that mighty city! for in one hour is thy judgment come."

– Revelation 18:10

"Do not attract attention to yourself in public. This is one of the fundamental rules of good breeding."

– Emily Post

THE WALL SPEAKS

She found herself leaning in, pressing her
Chin and her open hands against me.
She wept like Jesus, declaring the name
Of this city. Just as you live in the
Brain pan of your head, my consciousness, too,
Has *topos*. It lives within my chinks of
Moldering mortar, where the notes you leave
Petition me; I have seen them crumble,
But the questions illuminating them
Remain and tumble as if I were their
Rock polisher. As she leaned all her weight
On my steady, steady body, unmoved
In war or harvest, I reached through myself
To her, and she thought she heard Pyramus
Calling her name, but it was only me
Whispering the echo of her own voice,
Bouncing back loving cadence, for I do love her.
I love her more than you do, judging by the
Posters and the wheat paste you smother me
With now, right where she stood crying, and though

She too will molder in her *externa*,

I, neither internal nor external,

But the division of both of these, will

Find her repeated questions, petitions

Of her sobs, smoothly rubbing within me

As long as I stand here. They glow within

The cracks that weather has beaten into

Me over years of this assignment in

Your unweeded, mole-infested garden.

I make good neighbors, they say, even as

I inflict solitude. She killed herself

At my base, the plumb line being too straight

For her to imitate in uprightness.

Tear me down and cross to her unfettered.

PALMISTRY

You have been reading the lines
    Wrong.
        They go down, not up, not into
            The fingers from which flows the
                Blood when the meat is chopped
                Awry.
They drip down to the wrist,
    Which bleeds only when cut for
        The devil's dinner, not yours.
            The lines crawl vines into the
                Marsh waters of veiny rivers,
                    Not trees growing out of
                their banks.
They do bear fruit – bitter ones
    That fall mute into brackish
        Ocher of the skin's leather caress,
            Never in the fresh-picked-apple-in-the-
palm
                Sound of one hand
            clapping.

Yet they don't
    Damn, a watch synchronized
        With the doomsday clock, but
            The big hand tells the minutes,
                The big hand of the big Potter of
The big celadon ball on which we sit.
    But the little hand, that is your hand,
        Is blindly groping for Braille in
            The kiln-fired glaze to tell even one of the
                Hours.
They cannot tell you what you
Want to know.

PATMOS LYRIC 3

The people who exiled me did not know this island is inhabited. The natives look like me, only they live in still tidal pools into which I gaze. When I move, they move. I am in love with the one who visits me most to stare at me. Our eyes lock in perfect recognition.

This island, a walled rock garden, cloistered by crenellated waves, sits in the middle of a fallen world. I am the center of this universe, the monarch of all I survey, except my silent lover. Lava formations go ashy in the pool where he watches.

I dove in one day to embrace him, but he retreated deeper. I hit bottom. I stood up, my shoulders above the water. He had escaped somewhere. I searched the banks surrounding the pond, heard an albatross cry. I hate his coquetry. Once more, he alludes me.

AT THAT TIME IN THE CITY

At that time in the city, the ferry let off at a plaza. On that night, the lovers crossed for a concert on the other bank in the glass atrium filled with palm trees that grew coconuts during Ice seasons. A foreign singer was coming for her national debut. The critics pretended to understand her.

At that time in the city, after the ferry there were hot dog carts with clean-boiled dogs. The sodas of the lovers beaded sweat, even though the only hot thing was steam out of metal boxes where sausages bubbled. They waited for the foreign singer. They saw her saunter. Two foreigners – they could tell them by the way they shivered – asked her for an autograph and posed with her as the flash went off, and off, and off.

At that time in the city, any pair in love could sneak in a concert hall for a sound check. There had been no blood drive to search for weapons yet. The two lovers tiptoed inside behind the foreign singer. The sound check went:

> *One, two, three, four!*
> *Pencils, paper and glue and you!*
> *Tempers, pimples and strife --a knife!*

The two lovers did not comprehend any more than the critics, but neither admitted this. They were in love, this was an adventure, and at that time in the city, the bitterness had not yet descended in its fine, black powder that comes up to swim in the polluted summer.

> *Mic one, mic two,*
> *Anniversary marks the spot!*
> *Population control get shot!*

The foreign singer went backstage to change, and they rubbed noses alone in the atrium with the silent trees, no birds, just a faint mildew and the creak of green chairs. At that time in the city, lovers could sit nose-rubbing for hours on green chairs and forget about state schedules. The hours had not yet been dissected by the sponsors for thirty-second infotainment spots, not like today.

The lovers sat until the house opened. The foreign press and hip-swiveling *cognoscenti* who had read the reviews recommending this took programs and sleekly filed in, filled the green chairs three-quarters to the back of the palm-frond-strewn room. The lights dimmed. The lovers held hands. At that time in the city, lovers still held hands automatically in the dark, not at all like today.

> *Hello, named city!*
> *Sentimental handcuffs are locked!*
> *Gravitational pull half-cocked!*
> *This is Radio Free French Kiss!*
> *Take a number and flail amiss!*

The lovers squeezed each other's hands absent-mindedly as the foreigners – they could tell them by the way they danced on the rhythm – edged closer to the stage. At that time in the city, people thought concerts were happy, almost like political rallies without the lies and riot gear, not like today. The singer sang:

> *Bang! Slang! Spam! Dram!*
> *Pizza boxes and trash Tuesdays!*
> *Movies rented and flash flood haze!*
> *Ignore spouses in sports seasons!*
> *Slap the slut and the whore reasons!*

Years go by and the love fades black!
Blame the other one for slick slack!
Aging, raging and page one news!
Slugging, mugging and plug-in blues!

The lovers dropped each other's fingers. In the mildew, they smelled – was it wormwood concocted into absinthe? Was it a metallic smoke precursor of when all the buildings would burn down the year they would break up? – a sour smell, worse than the smell of the marijuana the foreigners – they could tell them by the way they stood aloof even when passing joints down the aisle, like no one would notice, like no police officer would arrest them after the show – were smoking, elbows on the stage, hands stretched toward the singer's skirts. The smell the lovers smelled, it was a chemical smell, a reaction to something plastic. At that time in the city, a person could go for hours without seeing anything plastic, except in the financial district, not like today. Then, places had not yet gotten strip-mauled, and the aluminum was brick historically preserved, not new epoxy.

Spinsters, Spandex and spleen spun out!
Twanging twinges and twist and shout!

Masturbation and massive guilt!
Pornographic on Amish quilt!
Loosey goosey and lung and gall!
Blinders winders and wood and wall!

At that moment in the city, in the song of the foreign singer being sung to the city, at that moment, that very moment in the stench, the lovers understood what critics had missed in the most insightful phrases of their articles in the *Times*. They knew they would not survive another season together because the city, even though at that time in the city it looked as solid as the skyscrapers, as healthy as the palm-fronds clean of any bird dung because no birds could fly through the atrium glass and nest there, the city, it would cough them up out of its diseased lungs and make them choose

Other dance partners, maybe the foreigners, who understood the new rhythms, seemed less mystified by the hocus-pocus words of hip new songs, and the city – at that time

In the city, people planned on living in the city forever, not like today – would make them forget each other. The concert would end. The style would change. The covenants – at that time in the city, there were covenants -- would shatter. The atrium glass would break when the concrete from above toppled on it, and the birds, well-meaning, with the cruel ice, would ruin the palm court, and the soot, the black powder that was the city's bitterness, would burst from the steam pipes below, where it had been waiting -- waiting in ashes, smelling of maggot-ground hot dogs and rancid, soggy contraband weed, and of each of the torn-up papers where newly met lovers write each other's numbers -- to erupt. The lovers knew this even though no one else, no *cognoscenti*, no critics, nobody in the city at all could understand the metaphors of the foreign singer, and quietly they crossed back over, left the concert before the encore.

AFTER THE GREAT SPEECH

The orator stepped away from the platform,
And though people wept and hugged one another,

They tossed just as they had trashed things before. They
Praised the rhetoric and rhythm of the fine Jeremiad,

But because heeding warnings requires sit-ups, thrift,
Apologies, pregnant pauses, penitence, and pain –

They called the words saintly but amended no plans.
And maybe the prophet preached false. Maybe Ides would

Just be the fifteenth again. Sometimes the fifteenth is
A pay day, isn't it? And the bags accumulated curbside.

Rats ate the garbage, bringing fleas, who spread
The plague, and yet the blackening buboes got blamed on

Popcorn lodged beneath the skin, on moles overexposed
To sunlight – not the cause the great speech decried.

The dying hallucinated the orator standing in a choir loft,
Pigeon-covered, statuesque, only alive crying.

Others gasped last breaths seeing his words flap above
Bat-like in Helvetica, folding and unfolding consonants.

Much later, after the mass graves got filled, the air wafted
Lemongrassy, leathery, not magotty, they made a plaque

Of the speech, fastened it to a shrine for the orator, and
Children wrote book reports about it, but nobody ever

Pondered it with the field trip over, the paper turned in,
The grade assigned. The text book moved on to the next
Chapter.

PATMOS LYRIC #4

I write this naked, crouching over sticks in
The mud. My flesh-sweat stinks of fish I net
In the shallows. I await Revelation –
When Christ crouched in the dust and wrote in the sand Near
The captured adulteress, He waited like this
For words to transform the dirt into a solid
Epistle. The woman wept. Men with rocks shifted
Weight, clenched and unclenched, copper and salt of
Blood on their tongues. But those earth clods understood
Waiting for language is a virgin pregnancy.
The surface seems inert, dire even, but when scratched
Just so, water and land get rightly divided.
The Creator proclaims in *Aleph, Bet*, "Light be,"
And behold, there is light. Rocks from clenched fists drop.
Woman loses her accusers. The ground upholds
Her bare feet running away.

ABOUT THE MUD

I can build a hut from mud. I can sculpt a
Man, if I am a god. Surely, I am one. I
Dwell and marry. I am not alone. Then

Clods harden under sun. Sundry pieces fall off
Works. The man loses his nose like a leper. The
Hut loses its Western Wall. I look for water

To muddle with Earth to repair, but I am not
So much god that I make it rain. Christ heals lepers,
But the mud crumbles under my praying touch.
Only deified enough to make a false man,

I pile bricks and play house. This is no family.
I serve mud pies for lunch. No one asks for seconds.
The neighbors, out for a Sunday stroll, see me hunched
In the front yard, crouching, covered in filth, wailing.

THE AGING BOND GIRL CALLS HER BEST FRIEND

It's pathetic, darling. Not long after I tried
To extradite him from Ibiza with scissor-kicks
And napalm, I started asking questions, Lemon Drop.
Tanning on the deck of an arch villain's race yacht
Actually, left me feeling slightly chilly.

Of course, I got a pedicure and forgot it.
I moved to Bangkok at the invitation of
An opium-dealing silk merchant, ran into
James again, used my jujitsu to bamboozle
Him, but I could not squeeze his head between my thighs
To the point of annihilation – I kneed him,
Leaving him breathing but without his secret watch.
I called M on it and asked for a job. She laughed,
Told me I was overqualified to chase spooks.
Ma Chérie, I can't quite imagine what hit me.
In Mombasa, I saw him yet again jogging,
Well -- on his way to explode a terrorist camp,
Feebly disguised as a German neurosurgeon. Ugh!

I must have felt sorry for him, honey – Why else?
Out of mercy, I aimed my blow gun only at
His crotch, but probably because he has left so
Many sirens disgruntled, he was wearing shorts
Made of Kevlar and anti-nuclear fibers.

And yet he never calls me! I've tried to move on!
He never really ages, and I'm in my late thirties –
Living on the estate of a blond Viennese
Wine merchant, feeding his peacocks cyanide chicken
Pellets and training his nubile teenage daughter
In aquatic ballet for the next Olympics.
To this day, my dearest, I've never really
Understood what we were fighting about, why I
Keep finding secretive men so entrancing, and
Even though I am still quite lovely for a girl
Of a certain age, I've never built anything
For myself. Well -- there is the valise of diamonds
I stole back in the late Seventies from that sheik –
I never delivered them to the handsome man
Who wanted to make the satellite to destroy
American missile silos, those rocks and the

Underground plastic explosives factory I
Opened with my ex-roommate Ludmilla in Prague,
But what does it all mean, my little butterfly?
Why keep going skiing in Gstaad? Why après ski?
Why keep getting thermal treatments at the Geller
Spa in Buda? Why keep polishing the same knives?
One day, I'd like to bake a pie without any
Rohypnol in the crust, just to see how it flakes.

THE ASTRONAUT'S WIFE

Without wishing to, I confide you to shadows
As I stare at the capsule slipping in orbit
Behind the chalky, round lamp inconstant, and I
Imagine you cradled in space, suckled by tubes,

Wordless as you curve back this way invisible,
The substance now of things hoped for later, not too
Much later, I hope, the evidence of things not
Seen, things seen soon, I hope against hope, and I wait

For your ricochet around, a seed I have sown
To come up greenly, but this winter night sky is
Blacker than any soil near Cape Canaveral,
And I wonder what you see on the other side,

Camouflaged from Earth, hidden from my telescope,
Muted from my ham radio. I refuse to
Ask if weightlessness tempts you away from me
To new missions further, further and further flung, if
The dark veil might snag, and you could stall mid-curve,

Plummet into a crater pockmarking night, but

Despite my clenched jaw, I squint up again, recall
Penelope, her wool tapestry woven and
Unwoven as her rogue Odysseus wandered,
And I look to the days' dishes, diapers, wonder
What might be the point of work while you are out of
Sight -- somewhere surely a *Star Trek* Circe offers
Her hospitality, turning spacemen to pigs
In space redundantly – but never out of mind.

THE SHARK AND THE BODYGUARD

At twelve, the ocean curls its muscles in a swell
When he allows himself to wander down the pier.
Inhaling the crab smell of night fishermen's

Buckets filled with pink crustaceans gasping their last,
He, the bodyguard, attempts to forget his day,
The near-misses, the bullet holes in the doorjamb

Above his head. He brings a woman or goes stag,
But at dusk, at Nathan's Hotdogs, he swallows it
All, and in the dark, only in the dark, he guards

Himself. One evening, after the Cyclones lose it
At the new ballpark, he lumbers down the long
Dead end, past the shattered waves, further still into

Deeper darkness, past sundry clinched lovers and the
Last babies awake, past gangstas bat-wing-hooded
Who avert their eyes as he languidly slinks by,

Down to the end where they speak only in foreign
Languages, the patois of Korean, Spanish
And lesser-known dialects of Atlantic air,

And with broad gests and exclamations, they explain,
"They have just caught a shark, down on the very end."
He strips a dollar off a heavy bankroll and

Palms it to the prophet of this news without a
Word. He makes a beeline for it. The shark lies there,
Its gills vainly undulating, and street urchins

Gingerly poke it with a fishing pole to watch
It writhe, its tail arcing like a bow bent, its trunk
Sidewinding like a cornered cobra defanged.

The bodyguard asks the fisherman how much for
It, and, given the price, he flips bill and bill in
The shad-gut hand, grabs the man-eater by the waist,

And flings it spinning into the dank waters. He
Watches to see if it floats. It does not. It swims.

The fin barely scalpels the surface, then descends.

The crowd, in the idioms of summer darkness,
Of Brooklyn's disappointed immigrant struggle,
Ask him, the bodyguard, why. He points in blackness

And says, "I save the lives of every comer,
Even of those bastards who deserve the smack-down.
It's just what I do. I can't stop working. Blame God.

"The shark is my brother, even if he wants to
Eat me. My clients, rich as they are, would eat us,
Too, to keep their wealth. I can't stop working. Blame God.

"Sometimes, Coney Island is a carnival hell.
Sometimes, like now, it is the kingdom of Jesus.
No one dies tonight. I can't stop working. Blame God."

MICROSOFT COMPANY PORTRAIT 1978 -- AND PROPHECY

I.
Yes, everyone that year owned too much
Italian Polyester. Farrah Fawcett
Managed to flip-and-giggle, but no one else.
      Contact lenses then floated rigid -- itchier
      Than a good pair of coke bottle glasses,
      Yes. But these twelve against the rumpus room

Wall in scruffy suburbia, sweating
Into a sofa while the photographer
Focused, denim-vested, embossed vinyl
      Pocket protectors, birds' nests for beards,
      Dumbo ears flapping like wings, something Wounded
      By the schoolyard bully in each gaze, something Crazed,

Craving substitutes for Unattainable
Cheerleader love left behind in a dust
Of disappointment during homecoming
      Week, the floats floating by with no hope of

    Waves from the queen, court, or even the drum
    Majorette corps, these twelve smashed together

For a moment torn from the screens they stared
Into, mad alchemists stoking glowing
Cauldrons, looking lost, smiling cautiously,
    Standing, squinting, the there and the then too
    Glaring, not daring to hope what the screens
    Blinking green might show soon in unison,

These twelve, with their bony bug-eyed prophet,
    They don't look big enough to hold their mustard
    Seed-sized germinating secrets, their secrets yet to
    Sprout.

II.
In winter, the brown patch of weeds doesn't
Look like tomorrow's tulips. Jesus died,
And his disciples ran away. An egg,
    Seen for the first time, looks the same
    As a skipping stone. It, the shape of birth,
    Is the same shape as a zero.

III.

No one remembers it, But mid-Seventies,
In a Harvard dining hall, Freshman Bill Gates
Removed his glasses, lay his tray on the
>   Linoleum, tapped on his glass with a
>   Teaspoon, and announced in his Western twang,
>   "I'm dropping out. I don't need the Yale game

"To tell me who wins. I don't like the ice
In Cambridge. All this sculpted paperweight
Erudition wastes my valuable time,
>   Time more valuable than anyone
>   Else's here, dollar for dollar. Like
>   Southie bruisers call it in the townie

"Pool hall: "Eight Ball, right corner pocket," then
Watch the ball roll in, I'm calling it today:
Stand back Wallstreetwalkers, Nobel Prizeniks,
>   Bookworms -- By the time I'm forty, I'll have
>   Out-earned your combined family fortunes,
>   Even counting all property lost gambling,

"drinking, and whoring since you landed at
Plymouth Rock, founded Jamestown, stole the land.
I'm so sick of your muscular-handshake,
> Bleached grin monopoly on the things you
> Grab, I've decided to sell things that can't
> Get grabbed, things you can't even imagine

"In your Daddy's-friend-wrote-recommendation-
Letter lives. I'm building more than one
Hacienda in the clouds, and each
> Will stay aloft like circling hawks, rising,
> Expanding, molting new wings." No one
> Remembers it, no one. after a stunned,
Preppie silence, everyone returned to their Jello.

IV.
Eureka! Come quickly, Watson, I need you!
I see stars! An idea -- Edison's
Light bulb -- pops above the head of the one
> Refusing to face facts. Those of us who
> Believe it can be done draw the future

In the air with our index fingers.

Like Da Vinci, Ezekiel, Jefferson,
Morse, and Whitman surely call it in some
Ponderous pool hall in eternity:
    "Eight ball, right corner pocket," then watch the
    Earth roll where commanded, I'm calling it
    Today: That's an egg. Leave it under a

Chicken, and you get another chicken.
Those onions you're stomping on right now in
The mud will be next spring's tulips. The man
    You kill will rise from the dead in three days.
    That prisoner you torture will be your
    President before you're eligible

For your pension. Those dozen mad scientists,
Badly dressed, unmoored unabombers,
Doctoring the headless, bodiless monster
    With the keyboard, they'll run the world, and that
    Littlest pip-squeak on the photo's edge

Will be the richest man in history.

No one remembers this, no one, but you,
You lucky castaway, I've been calling
You each morning. Your name is on my list!
  Perhaps you can't hear me over the din
  Of alarm clocks that wake you for someone
  Else's dream job, of the tired conductor

Announcing the stop where that desk chair you
Drop into each Monday waits sagging, of
The spin class coach screaming orders as you
  Remind yourself that sweating is supposed
  To help you lose, of the kettles whistling and
  The pipes whining in lonely walls closing
    In around you. Your name is on my list!
    No one remembers this, no one but me.
      I look to the left, look to the right,
        Look to the left again, sigh,
        Wonder whether
You'll find me before the gang plank gets pulled up.

PATMOS LYRIC #2

At night, I found out, the island freezes.
I lit fire behind a rock formation.
Wood was scarce, as scarce as other voices.
The wind bayed. The sand scratched. It gets so cold.
Then at last embers spat me out a spark.

The messenger stood at once in the glare.
I think he touched my beard. It swelled in waves.
I became wheat. Yes, he harvested me,
The first fruit separated from the tares.
As he threshed me against the black boulders,
Ground me into meal, I did not fly off
In the gale blusterings of this exile.

Words, drawn butter, water, egg, honey, yeast,
Bound together whatever was left in
Me and bubbled so that by noon under
The merciless sun, the ideas baked,
And I could start to tell you what I know.

PATMOS LYRIC #1

The first night here, the little bit of wine
I had smuggled in for communion, I
Drank, not because I was thirsty, but it
Seemed that this hollow chalk pile was its own
Bone feast, the salt water a more honest
Rendering of false tears offered at the
Last Supper mimed with the parsley sprig dipped
In it to represent past worries. But
His blood? I look down at my scarred limbs still
Smelling of boiling oil, and I know that
The lone transubstantiation is me
Here. *Ecce Homo*, saved for service, a pot
Where water serves distant wedding guests
Miraculously, and my wounds, not His,
Evidence enough of resurrection –
After all, I have survived to write this.

THE THIRD SEAL

"And I saw the woman drunken with the blood of the saints, and with the blood of the martyrs of Jesus: and when I saw her, I wondered with great admiration.

– Revelation 17:6

"Mr. Kindhart, sitting next to you, says gently, 'Cheer up, little girl, it doesn't really matter!' And then you know to the full how terrible the situation is."

– Emily Post

THE METHOD

A metal bar under his tongue, the method
From the old regime, and they burned his gums with
      The juice from the car battery. His
      Mouth swelled – he had the mumps, they told Guards

When they put him back in solitary, and
He could not object. He smelled like gas burning
      Rubber, but then he had not bathed for
      Lack of water in days. What the other

Guards did not know they did not venture to guess.
The method worked like a charm that way. After mumps,
      And the other welts, the suicides,
      They did not think about them, either. The

Howling down the hall, that did not belong in
The answer to the question asked at the door,
      "How was your day, Hun?" Kiss. Kiss. And so
      Certain things that happened never happened.

The method worked like a charm that way. In his cell,
He knelt, clasped hands, but prayer was a spoken thing,
      And his tongue cauterized was as good
      As cut out. The silence of his smoked flesh –

Its wounds in oaken blossoms along his back
In cigarette-lighter rosary beads -- was
      His only litany. The gangrene
      In his gaze that turned maggoty, it screamed.

WHAT I AM NOT WRITING

A bad confession brings the curse, the cops, the paparazzi.
The word gets swallowed not to explode out. It becomes a
Firecracker pocketed,
A wafer that is a bone under the tongue, a "no,"
A "never," An "I hate you," An "I wish I were dead or
Killing you" –
It implodes and releases its germ warfare inwardly.

I go to the church basement for Bible study, but the
Facilitator whispers.
She tells me to hush. "These are new believers, babies in The
    Word,"
And you will confuse them. You will scare them. God is Simple.
Don't complicate.
"I know your heart. Your heart is good, but the question
You ask" – that question is pernicious, the aftertaste of
Prayers unanswered.

The catechism asks a question, gives a single response.
Comforters hypothesize

Secret sins. Don't ask questions of God, they say.
God will ask you things, too, and you cannot have the Answers,
       and then you will just look foolish, and when Your wife
       asks you, "Why don't you curse God and die?"
She has no malice, really.
She just wants to know why you don't, honestly.

What do you think He is thinking? When you write Something
down, that's your testimony. "Is it your Testimony, Miz
Williams, that on the night in question, the Defendant came to
       your door in a sulfuric cloud, but Passed by, since in
       silence, you had taken the switch you
Use to whip your grandchildren when they misbehave and
Streaked the door with the meat you butchered?"

I am not writing any of this down. The destroyer is off the
Record. The post gets deleted, the inquirer unfriended. The
Notepad only records groceries to buy, checks, chores
Crossed off after they are done. Still scrawled, un-exed
Remains this list:

"Write a brilliant dissertation; Exercise and floss daily; Take vitamins; Ask God that question; Bow; Ask again; Bow; Answer His questions one by one;

"Say to Him, unlike Job, 'Magnificent as you are, you
Really didn't explain it;' Bow;
Write down what He tells you. Ask for clarification; Bow;
Ask how that is good enough;
Make a fist;
Unclench your grip, and stare into your empty palm;
Stare harder; Bow;
Ask God if you can see His pattern of things; Ask why not;
Stare down at your knuckles;
Ask if you can trace His Hand like a Thanksgiving turkey;
Trace your own hand instead."

TRIBULATION LYRIC #3

My friends say it's so much easier –
They put their hand under the black scanner
And take what they like from the department.
At the doctor, the night nurse touches their
Forehead, not for fever, but for it, and
In the Braille there, she palpates the accurate
History. Who could oppose this, you ask?
I am trading tubers today under
The tarp. If they catch me, the gulag guards
Keep a long cot waiting, and they will drill
It into my skull by force. Even if
You don't want the spuds, don't point to me, please.
Why do I resist the arrest, you ask?
There are parts of me that are still holy.

THE CENTER

The exit is total. We never re-enter.
We patrol periphery, dreaming of center.

A book told me I was just an imitation
Of a mirage, a donut creaming its center.

Another book told me I had fallen years ago
In snakes, slithering a ring, screaming at center.

I burn my books. One tells the truth. All others lie.
God is light, parades in flames seeming at center.

The ashes go so well with sack cloth this season.
Fashonistas strike poses, preening at center.

Film replaces books; incinerated text goes flat.
Subtitles gibber through the screenings at center.

I find an unburned book hidden in a desk drawer.
In it, we all get redeemed, bringing us center.

Who, though, can return to the Hammurabi code?
Heads roll, executioners flinging them center.

We touch kisses on the Torah with blood-stained hands.
We kaddish all our victims, singing them center.

Yet, He is the Word made flesh, unimmolated,
And I scribble the smokeless meaning at center.

We cannot crawl back in the uterus, my friend
Nicodemus. New hope is gleaming at center.

Bereft of folio, our winter is ending.
New text shoots forth in green ink, springing at center.

Pardon, Jehovah, our elegies. They are jazz.
Find Anne B's Big Band, bopping, swinging at center.

THE UNBORN

I.

And Hannah answered and said, No, my lord, I am a woman of a sorrowful spirit: I have drunk neither wine nor strong drink, but have poured out my soul before the LORD… out of the abundance of my complaint and grief have I spoken hitherto. – 1 Samuel 1: 15-16

At the altar, I   imagined the five
of you – my fingers   splayed into the next
generation, stretched   palpating, and like
fingers, I could count   you all on one hand,
that is if you would   stand still now for the

family photo   –   *Wake up, my Tima!*
Maha, I told you   *leave Dawood alone!* –
Yusuf, let me help   *you with your hair; it's*
sticking up again.   *No, for the thousandth*
time no, this is our   *Christmas card, and no,*
it's just you and me   *and your father, it's*
just all of us. Stand   *still. Look straight ahead.*

I help Sarah with
I feel the pull of
burning against my
on my thumb tips that
You disappear, my

This is the only
Ever pose for, my
Treasures I have hoped

There is no marker
You. There is no red
no medical waste
were you corpses nor
nor miscarriages –
of justice, my dears.
to the police. This
will never appear

I have buried you
these papers, smudging
jet the printer spits.

her tights as she squirms.
the nylon slightly
palms, leaving a mark
disappears too soon.
imagined blessings.

photograph we will
beloved ones, my
for enduringly.

where I have buried
biohazard bin,
canister. Neither
mourned abortions,
perhaps miscarriage
I cannot complain
Christmas photo
on a milk carton.

here, in the folds of
your cheeks in ink
You are caught in the

tangles of x and the lower t, snagged
on the c without cedilla, on the
consonants of the cop who might ask me,
"And where exactly did you last see them?"

I have last seen you here. This is my last
glimpse, beloved ones, smelling of milk and
white glue, of yellow tempera paint and
pee. This is where the guards drag you off. I
tangle in the barbed wire against which I weep.

I have no right to mourn you, the unborn.
And yet I look at the bloody writing
in the lines of my palm, and I read in
the ancient Hebrew, the koph, the daleth,
and the shin from "Kaddish." The branch ends.

II.

If we have no peace, it is because we have forgotten that we belong to each other. – Mother Teresa

How dare I lament you, you who have never come into the world, when all around me, there are those who crave something unoffered? I visit the foundling home to hold a workshop, but what I need to do is grab every baby out of its bassinette, raid the orphanage and the animal shelter and leave with an army of babies, and puppies, and kittens, and troubled teens.

The teens hotwire a caravan, and we join, we make a circus. We eat weenies around some backwood camp fire, and we tell ghost stories –

The ghosts of the parents who left cigarette burns on the arm of this one, the ghost of the father who touched this one there, and there, and there while the mother stood by and did nothing. We think of new songs to sing, ones that have happier lyrics than the other ones on the radio, and we make up jokes where the punch lines make no sense, but we laugh so hard the soda comes out our noses.

But there is only so much money.

Even if there were money, there is only so much time.

Even if there were money and time, there is only so much me. I am not a loaf or a fish, and Jesus has not divided me after giving thanks. I am no meal for five thousand hungry ones.

I am barely a single happy meal.

I bake cookies for the neighbors on holidays. I leave notes.

They don't thank me. It's a rough neighborhood.

They probably don't eat the cookies.

Who can you trust these days?

Outside the garden, there are razor blades in apples everywhere.

III.

...Daughters of Jerusalem, weep not for me, but weep for yourselves, and for your children. For, behold, the days are coming, in the which they shall say, Blessed are the barren, and the wombs that never bare, and the paps which never gave suck. – Luke 23:28-29

I have been prudent. I have not brought out
a person in time of war or downturn.
No one at breakfast has glared at my booth
because spilt milk brought on crying over.
I never get glares in aisles because a
child has gone limp to wail or get a spanking.
I have not become a statistic or
a burden on the Republic or church.
I give charity. I don't receive it.

I have been quite sure, terribly cautious.
No one has been at all inconvenienced.
My bedroom is warm, tidy, and with my
Debt measurable. I am wise, quite wise.

Because look out there, out on that screen, around that corner, and in the drain pipes, and you'll see the PCBs and the rock-throwing

Palestinians, and some Irish Republican Army, and ISIS, and Russia, and the scandals, the matted hair, the teeth of the skull they just dug up, and the polar bear who is hungry, and swims to his death. The Janjaweed brandishes his machete. The girl has acid burns on her face. The boy has no arm.

The price of cream is rising. No one needs another suckler, do they?

And yet, let me show you their picture.

IV.

"…Rachel envied her sister; and said unto Jacob, Give me children, or else I die." – Genesis 30:1

Yusuf leans against the wall
As I type his non-existence.

His arms are brown branches of an olive tree.
When he colors, he makes green and black circles on the Page

"Ma! Look!" He lifts skyward the fruit from his fingers.
His head is slightly curly, coarse to my lips as I kiss.

I inhale scents of vegetation and clean boy sweat.
No matter how much I feed him, he stays skinny –

The sandwiches stretch him upwards, and I wonder
If he will be hanging from the hoop one day on

The court, or if some force will chop him down. I hear
The buzz saw. I turn to look over my other shoulder.

The crayons are gone, the butcher paper is blank.

I turn back. There is no shadow of him left.

I am in my apartment, a roommate only, no scuffs from
Size two sneakers anywhere to track his path away.

V.

No one is scouting for them anymore but me.

The search party has been called back in from the storm.

The investigation is cold cased. Only I am

Leaving the pictures posted everywhere:

The frame with question marks over ovals,

And I am asking if you have seen them, if

You can draw them you might be an artist,

And if you will let me know as soon as they arrive.

The one in the corner, that looks like Munch's screamer,

That's me.

VI.
Sarah won't get out of bed.

First I grab her face and kiss it. She mumbles and squirms.
Her eyes stay shut. Even though that beatific sleep caste

Has left the mask of her cherubic face, that sleep that looks
Like heavenly reward to which we may all return one day

If our lives have been right, unlike mine, which fills up the
Air with lies like these lines, but Sarah, an imagined thing,

She is safe if not saved, and she rolls on her stomach,
Knowing that this is only stalling the inevitable.

I call her name, intoning, "Sa-oo-rah! It is a school day!"
And so it is – even though she is only enrolled in my

Imagined classroom, and she moans, "No!" I leave
The room, pour milk in her plastic cereal bowl, sprinkle

It with berries, and again I return to the bed, where

Sarah is attempting to hide under the covers.

It's as if I can't see her at all under the bunched-up
Duvet. Again I lament, "Sa – oo – rah!" This is

The she-wolf in the dark howling for her pups,
Her icescape call, and she waits in the silence.

I lift up the quilt, sure I'll see the footless pink
Flannel with the balloon clusters printed all over,

But she must be up. I check bathrooms, listening for
Sinks left running after the Snoopy toothbrush

Bristles. Where is she?

VII.

At birth? At conception?

No! Much sooner than that, or much later.

Life begins when the women sits alone, perhaps even as a virgin, perhaps in a place where no one knows her and she is forever anonymous, and she says to herself, "there should be another. I will give her pause."

The hollow expands, sometimes until it is the size of an island, and the woman hangs a hammock up between two palm trees and rocks waiting.

The hollow says, "Be it done to me according to your word." It is done, but not according to her word, never according to her word precisely, but it is done.

VIII.

Maha has taken the seat cushions off
The two couches and built a fort. She peers

Out between the blue upholsteries, makes
The sound of bullets whizzing, empty wind.

Maha is impersonating a warrior princess today.
She just learned the word revenge – or thinks so.

"I am The Revenge!" She shouts, or am I
Hearing the argument on cable news

From the next room? "I am The Revenge, Ma!"
She rustles between the pillows like change

Lost in the lint, the remote hidden where
I sit uneasily, wishing to flip

Infomercials but cannot find the box.
I dig in the cracks of the soft spaces,

Expecting to tickle her, The Revenge.
I dig and dig and dig and dig and dig.

It's funny how things disappear like that.
Maha is missing, The Revenge vanished.

IX.

The week after September 11th, after having calmly leading the evacuation of the nearby building where I worked, after losing my job the very next day in a layoff, I lay restless at home, cat-napping. I dreamt I was in the rubble with an empty baby carriage, a white mask over my mouth, digging for them, gagging.

X.

Sophia doesn't know how to read yet,
But she has taken one of my textbooks,

One that explains insanity in
Post-war protagonists, a banned book, no --

Wait, hang on -- I think I mean a burned book,
And she is flipping through the pages that

Are covered in the cuneiform she
Can't comprehend – do I mean "burned" or "banned"?

"Ma! I'll tell you what it says!" She grabs my
Leg and hugs it, yes, I'm sure she hugs it.

I feel the weight of her. "What does the book say?"
I hear pages turning under my desk.

"Sophia? What does the book say?" I hear
Crying. Yes, I hear my own voice crying.

XI.

"I want to pursue that subject you mentioned to me when you were last here, and to show you that I am not all stone." – Charles Dickens

There's another one missing —Well, missing?
I don't think I miss him. "Waled! Waled!"

He has a theme song. It's in Arabic,
and that song – I play it all the time, not
thinking about him, because I wouldn't
let him steal the song along with the rest.

In the live recording, they are shouting
another Arab name, "Waled! Waled!"

Waled is a pop star in Lebanon.
The one I don't miss, his name might just be
Waled. How would I know? The name on his
passport, green card, driver's license -- all fake.

The FBI, Interpol, NSA –
They might just miss him. They call him missing.

The drums roll. Violins moan. I think the
crowd is in a park in Beirut. They shout,
"Waled! Waled!" They love, they miss Waled.

The Queens County DA gave him a file
number. I had a taffeta dress made.

I hear a male voice moon-howl digitized.
It whispers like a wraith autotuned.
He's whispering in my ear,
"أم أولادي, *mère de mes enfants*."
The crowd in Beirut chants "Waled! Waled!"
I don't know any Waled. I just know
music. Music plays. Waled sings to me.

The NSA took over that file. I had
the invitations printed in light green.

I know how to belly dance like a bride
at her own wedding in Beirut. I can,
and I do. The best part about belly
dancing: I can do it without partners.

The real Waled starts to sing in Beirut.
I undulate. I tremble, a tent in
a sandstorm. I once owned finger cymbals.
I used to wear a big ring. The finger
cymbals got lost when I moved. My ring left
with him, the one who might be named Waled,
too, for all I know. The account emptied.

The FBI is calling again. He
demanded more. They trace some old transfers.

I am still dancing. I fling my long hair
around, forgetting him, but not my hopes.
Osama Bin Laden got shot.
The one that was not named Waled,
The one who is not on this recording,
A secular song, the kind the Osamas of the world
Hate, the one that makes me shake,
The one that is not this singer Waled,
"Waled! Waled! Waled!" He is at large.
Waled the singer croons to me.

I jut my right hip out, then back, then out.

The local police advise me to get
a handgun. They guarantee me nothing.

I should look for ammunition, but I'm
dancing. I'm dancing forward. He did not
get away with those lingering bass notes.
the song in the air – yes, I still own that.
I am still undulating and trembling.

He's still out there.
He has my social security number.
He has my photograph.
He has my address, notarized documents.

I am still undulating and trembling.
I still own this rhythm. I still own it –
What I thought would be – it's still mine.
I am still undulating and trembling.

XII.

There are one million new children forced into sex slavery every year. I give a few hundred dollars to free a dozen of them. That's all it costs – a few hundred dollars. I wait for when they will send me the package containing them, but I don't ever get a box with holes drilled in it in the mail.

My mother never knew me. She saw me every day murkily through an etching in her head of another girl, not a naughty girl, a girl who cared about things she said I did, a girl who would have nodded when she said, "But you WANT to go to uncle Bill and aunt Jen's house!" -- That girl. This was a girl who wanted to do well in girl math class so she could get a girl good job one girl day. She would have waited until. She would have worn hemlines lower. She read Alfred Lord Tennyson's "The Mermaid," and thinking of hemlines, she repeated to herself his "lowadown, lowadown." This girl did not think nice girls did the girl things I did.

One day I was grounded because my mother had a dream about the real me. It was my fault. I was her nightmare. The other girl thought this was entirely fair, and like a good girl, she refused to stay in the girl room with me where I was punished. I did not miss her, turned up the music, waited for them to box me up in the big carton with all the holes in it, waited for the clerk to scan the bar code, forward me to the next spot for tracking.

XIII.

Dawood helps me decorate cupcakes. He holds
The green sprinkles and the red hots away

From his chest, radioactive materials.
He turns canisters upside down and shakes them.

He sounds dropping bombs – the red hots napalm.
The green sprinkles strafe the chocolate glaze.

Then, having run out of desserts, just or unjust,
He moves to the rest of the table, covering

The table cloth with Christmas day carpet bombing.
"That's enough, Dawood!" I scold. He looks up just once,

Does the math gaze determining the ratio
Of how mad I am to how much trouble awaits,

And he continues, "No, Dawood! Stop it!" I grab at him,
But he is out of reach. The carpet bombing bombs

On. Chocolate spreads, covering the table now.
He is out of reach. "I said to stop it, Dawood!"

But somehow, like stealth bombers we send to
Arab world countries, where children get named "Dawood"

Instead of "David," Dawood disappears in dark
Frosting, leaving me holding canisters I have emptied

Onto cupcakes I have baked for no one at all
To take to a birthday party for the unborn.

XIV.

My friend Deborah, who lived in a condo near Ground Zero back in 2002, held a baby shower. While she opened gifts with little tunics, little sling shots, little sandals, little scrolls, I glanced between ribbon cuttings over my shoulder out the window and watched them hauling away pieces of charred iron i-beams turned into curly fries in barges headed for Fresh Kills and parts beyond.

We "oohed. " She grinned proudly. This condo blew centralized air conditioning temperatures on us, but still we went outside on the roof winter garden and saw from there the smoking hole left where the towers had stood. We needed our coats up there. It was chilling to the bone.

When the baby was stillborn, they had a memorial service to her – a baby girl -- on that roof garden, now sprouting, except for her. I hugged Deborah. She wailed.

I told her, "God will reward you for your patience this day."

What a blasphemer I was. God forgive me.

After the reception, I walked down to the loading point of the barges and looked in the box car of concrete being hauled away.

Ours weren't in there, either.

XV.

Fatima is my baby, my youngest one of all.

When she goes off to college, my work will be done.

I change her diapers now. I find them empty.

She curls up on the changing table, grabbing her toes and trying

To stick them in her mouth while I hum to her

The song is – what is the title again? Something about swans.

She gurgles back to me cheerfully.

The baby wipe is blank, no signs of rash, either.

I sprinkle talcum powder on her, much too much,

The white container hiccups a cough of white

Dust and Fatima, my baby, my last one, is

Assumed into it, a holy virgin rising, as it dissipates.

XVI.

Here are some fortune cookie secret messages from Headquarters:

Due to female infanticide
When you reach a fork in the road, take it.

There are thousands of missing baby girls.
You will hear today from an old friend.

The men find a void when they look
Your secret admirer will soon appear.

For someone to walk Forbidden Palace Grounds with.
Your lucky number is two.

They crack open these biscuits, and hope to find.
You can depend on the trust of the collective.

Gentlemen, I've already searched there – fortune cookies aren't even Chinese, really, and as for the missing women, every time I think I've found one, I see it is just my own reflection in the mirror staring back at me.

XVII.

"Those lines that I before have writ do lie,
Even those that said I could not love you dearer." – Sonnet LXV

You have read my five fingers, their whorled prints,
and yet when police		detectives dusted,
they saw the ghosts of		no touches at all.

You have read my palm.		The lines curl downward,
a slippery slope,		and I am fallen.
No one cares but me		about the unborn
misbegotten ones		I have invented,
and why should they		when they hear other cries,
have children of their		own to educate?

I have no marker but		these words, no stone or
flower to leave at this		memorial, just
this requiem of ink.		Other mothers have
children they have just		imagined, ones they
never understand		but think they do, ones
they have pretended		exist, but these ones,
unlike mine, have an		incarnation on
which to project the		impossible plans.

I have loved you, my unborn ones, more than
I have ever loved the living or dead.
You are the best of my aspirations.
You are the peace I leave in the wreckage.
I have failed you in failing to have you.
How can I grow old without you grown up?
This age has left me with a smoldering black hole.
The barges ship the beams to Fresh Kills, and I
Remain here in false bereavement.
They will rebuild it over my ashes.

THE FOURTH SEAL

"Thine heart was lifted up because of thy beauty, thou hast corrupted thy wisdom by reason of thy brightness: I will cast thee to the ground, I will lay thee before kings, that they may behold thee."

– Ezekiel 28:17

"Whether we Americans are drifting toward or from finer perceptions, both mental and spiritual, is too profound a subject to be taken up except on a broader scope than that of the present volume. Yet it is a commonplace remark that older people invariably feel that the younger generation is speeding swiftly on the road to perdition."

– Emily Post

SCREEN PLAY

To film the scene in the cemetery where
I peer into my mother's open grave
And curse at her descending mahogany coffin,
Fist shaking, violins swelling,
Eloquent dialogue and
Oscar-caliber performances, a thumbs-up, a must-see,
They will take
Astroturf, cover over a hundred
Styrofoam mounds,
And carve marble tombstones, each engraved with a Fake name,
And they will sprinkle rain on my fake face to look
Just enough like tears,
And they will make mud out of modeling clay and streak
My manicured hands,
And they will paint mascara circles under
My color-contact-lens eyes
And they will hire a professional to smear my lipstick
Hysterically,
And they will turn on a million blow dryers all at once in a
Roaring unison

So that my platinum wig waves like a battle flag,
And they will hire a hundred actors at Equity minimum
And dress them in black Dacron and
Lycra, the best from wardrobe,
Let them keep their sunglasses on from home, but
Fake the rest of it --
Silk and plastic flowers,
A rabbi who doesn't even speak
Hebrew -- he'll be Mexican -- not Hassidic,
And a faint loop recording of bird sounds in the Background.

But the truth was that
I really did curse in my head as your redwood box
Took the down escalator and
I threw the fist full of fragrant dirt clods
The rabbi handed me -- You claimed lately to be
Jewish, despite priests' protests --
Under bright sunlight, and
I wore my sunglasses from home,
And a black linen suit, no synthetic fibers, worthy of a
Kennedy mourning.
But the truth was the flowers were

Fake -- not the petals, but the sentiment --
I shook hands, heard every
Guest tell me your story over and over,
A faint loop in my head, as I listened minimally.
As they paused, I said to each on cue, my lipstick Unfeathered,
    my voice
Faint and wistful,
"Thank you for telling me that about her."
But the truth was
I would have celebrated your departure, the way
I did every time
When you left me in a huff at the dormitory,
Alone in the room with the boy at last,
Calling me a dirty whore on your
Stomping strut out the dirty door,
When you hung up the phone on me,
Your silence the greatest blessing you could bestow,
But the truth was
The camera really was pointed at me now,
The sky yawning wide and
Humming like a vacant, white screen,
The churning flip, flip, flip of

Your last reel ended still audible from the projection room.

DECEIT OF MUSICALS

In each film, Gene Kelly dances with another girl.
He also proposes to each, or implies that
    He will soon. I wonder
    If they each knew about
    The others. Would Leslie
    Caron have taken off
    A ballet flat and whacked
    Him over his brill-creamed
    Coif? Judy Garland knew,
    Suspected, or she guessed.
    She took drugs as she sang
    "Get Happy." The drag queen
    Favorite Debbie what's-
        Her-name from *Singin'*
        In the Rain – She just made
        Her daughter go postal
        From the edge for revenge,
        And Rita Hayworth left
        The great film genius to
        Play *Cover Girl* with him.

Orson went lunatic
And sold wine, not art,
    But still he dances in,
    Dances out, spinning a
    New partner whenever
    The music shifts its beat.
    Hollywood lies to me.
    I eat chips on the couch.
    I wonder how this has
    Happened to me again.

BOTTICELLI AFTER SAVANAROLA

Burnt offerings are sin offerings – How have I offended?
These frolics,
Can they have blocked the light of your landscape
More than those damned seductive
Rantings of hate evangelized, of Wisdom
Herself raped and cast underfoot like a smashed idol?

And those erstwhile-naked beauties, the ones my youth
Once beckoned, that pose for me
Still posthumously after my second glass of wine taken
With a dinner of smoked game and bitter
Herbs, svelte glories turned to dissipated fumes,
How have they, so nubile and firm,

Transgressed more than my own
Three-dimensional contemporary flesh
Surviving them only to dimple and
      Sag? Not the lovely scallop-riding
      Surfers, not the preening musclemen,
      Crouching and flexing between the pines,

    But my own penitent meat deserves
    The scourge of the burlap shirt, the
    Self-flagellation of the private cell,
    The lit torch thrown at the stake!

    And how will anyone know who I
    Have truly been, with all my relics
    Having shared the fate of the Library at
    Alexandria, the Viking-raided abbeys,
    And the pretty ones who posed for me?
My sullen Madonnas now are all masked Minervas,
My weeping Jesus an Apollo wearing a false beard.
These reactionary times drape all things in sackcloth
And ashes, and the new ruins dug through produce
Nothing but the melted holocaust stinking of
Immolated pigments, arson and regret.

LINER NOTES

The album jacket contains dust inside that smells like the year the record was pressed. Is that cardamom? Myrrh? Fish blood from a cooler sat in a trunk? Sweat? Or just jazz? These are the liner notes for this waxwork, the cire perdu *that has rendered this shape, this ekphrasis on the page. The photo is in grayscale. The white singer wears pearls.*

"When I started crooning,
I never thought I would work with
The Four Horsemen. Like
Everyone in the scene,
I read their reviews, heard covers, but had never 'digged'
Them live.
But these cats blew my mind when
I caught them live at the
Blue Note. I never saw a band tear
Up a crowd like that – overturned tables, bleeding waiters,
Bartender beheaded.

"I knew I had to cut a disc with them, a buzz saw Blade Rolled
away from its roots. I offered them
The sacrifice of the mutilated doll.
It was wild, our first jam session.
Now that they all went home to their maker in that horrific
Plane crash outside of Memphis, I
Have to take stock of how they influenced my current Sound.
Who am I?

"My sorority sisters of swing,
Peggy Lee and Sandra Dee, Doris Day, the polite girls –
They wouldn't recognize this growling.
I don't see them at club dates any more.
They think I'm on smack like
Lady Day, but I'm just hipper, thinner than I was in those
Nancy Drew sweater set days.
The Chi Omegas have blackballed my lyrics.
They say

"I sing like a Cosmo girl, but it's not
Orgasm that drives this howling.
It's more primeval

Than something as temporary as sex or death.
It's jazz that comes from self-flagellation. If
I have one message to my fans, it is repent.
The days grow shorter. I was sitting in on a
Recording session with the
Whore of Babylon, and she is ready to wail like a tenor sax.

"You cats need to dig -- wax turns to vinyl, vinyl turns to
Tape, tape turns to lasered plastic, and
Plastic turns to the ineffable, and the ineffable
Turns to the sudden
Digitized evaporation of all the innocence you cling to.
We are entering an era where
Singers have to face it:
There are no hits, only blows to the head, so get ready!
Meanwhile, I thank you for listening.
I hope you enjoy these tunes.
Lots of love."

CONCERT

From his balcony seat, he looked across
Other niches, but no ticket-holders
Would meet his gaze. The mezzanine below

Outmanned his velvet box, seemed disinclined
To gawk above. Hadn't they played fanfares
When he entered? Hadn't the spotlight lit?

With their back to him, he clenched his dentures.
The orchestra tuned, toned plucking, bowing
The odd string, the weighty gold drapes shut.

Hadn't he made himself the world's *maestro*?
The piece they played was contemporary.
The baritone sang of snatching at straws.

The sopranos screamed "Nevermore!" Only
Then did he catch one man's eye at long last –
A wizened man, wheelchair section, a full

Decade older than even he, vulture-
Eyed, a reaper finger crooked and pointed
Malediction from the front row at him.

THE END OF SINGING

He said the singing ended because in
evolution, humans all became tone deaf
To enhance their sense of smell. This idea got
      Applauded at cocktail parties. The professors
      Disagreed – man had stopped singing because it
      Grew obvious that singing changed nothing, and

Market trends pointed to new sublimations.
The church declared no, hymnals had disappeared
Because texting was much more convenient;
      No need nearer my God to thee when the number
      Could be typed with holy thumbs.
      The singing ended,
      Fashion Week claimed, because hemlines rose Exposing

Mouths muter than the old modes, and tunes were
The old black, not the new black, anyway. White House
Press Secretary Melody McGee declined
      To name names but claimed lyrics would be
      Banned next year.

    The Meat Packing
    District bars clinked glasses and joked
    Over no music – only louder and louder

Slogans.
Soon, the richer people forgot even
"Happy Birthday" and
"Jingle bells, Batman smells," but
Out in the back yard on an unusually
    Warm day in February a young mother hummed
    As she shook out a quilt to catch the clean air of
    The Mississippi morning, and she didn't care
    That no one but
    Her daughter and the dog heard her.

SUBTERRANEAN LYRIC #1

And I just got to tell you
I do intend
To stay closer than any friend. – Bob Dylan

Throw no bones to divine my message. Find me here, past the
Shakespeare-in-the-Park
Ticket line that punctures the
Great Lawn with the heels of Manhattan's
Drama queens, past the fountain where the pudgy
Angel looks like a milk maid,
Surrounded by the underfed roller jockeys, past the men
Mid-chess on stone benches,
Past the elders tossing their
Baci balls in sublimation of things gone,
Past the runners running around the water and
Forgetting the falcon that cannot see the falconer,
Over here, beneath your blistering tarsals, still sentient. See?
I have scattered a letter in muddied leaves across grass that
Canopies me. I have taken tadpoles

In the tourist pond, trained them to croak one night as frogs next
    season in
Morse code to you.
That hot dog cart rattle is a staccato imploring still that you
Would finally, finally hear me.
Last year's acorns fell like folktale crumbs to where you
Must stroll. Yes, here, this is the patch.
Lie down on your stomach above where
I have hidden, and spread your arms.
Embrace grass, one ear to the earth, and listen.
Stay an hour; you will swear you have heard me knocking.

SNAILS

Have you ever wondered how they make them?
They scoop escargots from slime pits out back,
      Throw them in cauldrons, add flour, cover
      And wait two days while the treble slither

Gnaws the white wheat refined. Snail guts pass muck
Until the snarl of them poop lily white.
      Cleaned out, they creep toward frying pans,
      Butter and garlic *à la bourguignonne*.

I have been moving too slowly these days,
Though I meant to catch up with the new pace.
      The starch in my diet, no fresh greens,
      Bloats me. Shelled in race privilege, boxed in

By bags, instead of choppering rescue missions
Airlifting you, dark moods overwhelm me
      Self-indulgently. I putter around.
      My close friends urge me to give him a chance.

For the sake of this nation. I will try.

They are sure he will make us great again.

  I smell something burning at a distance.

  I hear things clatter. I see a great light.

SUNBURN CUISINE

The sun hammers my glassine skin. July
Brims its cauldron with wet soot while crawfish
Like me hide pickpocketing oxygen
From rising bubbles, balloons escaping
State fairgrounds, abandoning me in the
Stinking swamp to keen as my bones whistle.

Flesh simmers into a delicacy
For obese deities. The kaddish card
The Riverside Memorial Chapel
Handed me lies in state in my recipe
Card box between Cajun dirty rice and *étoufée*.
It anticipates your big day.

My English falls in chopped cooking
Imperatives, crawfishing for Hebrew,
Latin, or any dead language which can
Express bon voyage sentiments. Good-
Bye to you will be polite, a business
Cocktail departure, shaking each right

Hand as I leave, preceded by nothing
But small talk. We have not exchanged cards
Or promised to do lunch these thirty years,
But my adieu will sound regretful.
I know how to work a room.

Lemon squeezed over my head bleaches streaks down it.
Lemon clenched between my teeth whitens my smile.
Lemon drizzled over my flesh shrinks my blemishes.
Lemon makes crawfish taste so much sweeter.

I drink lemonade in the heat. My skin
Ripens into a blood tangerine. The sun
Screen slips all over me like *beurre blanc*,
Adding fat and fragrance, but protecting
Me not at all. When I stop banging
Against the lid and howling, and my
Hide screams the red of my wounds, that's when
You'll know I am ready for you.

THE DRUNKEN MONORAIL

The train rounds mountains rakishly. The tunnels
Release their hungry bats in a black confetti.
The second-class passengers are handcuffed to the
Luggage rack so the conductor can catnap.

Between stations, in the club car, a pink sow gets
Trapped in a Plexiglas aquarium. She squeals
Invectives. The tuxedoed bar tender spritzes
With a soda gun, buckets of boiling water

To drown her. She becomes a blonde Ophelia,
Pouts in red lipstick and the pearls cast before her.
Eau non potable; Pig soup with flotsam and jetsam
Bubbling to the surface like so much cruel gossip.

Watch your pocketbooks. We're entering llama country.
Smell the night air through the cracked windows.
Between the
Guano and the boiled bacon, can't you catch a whiff of it --
The savage scent of our final destination?

SKIING IN IRAN

Black wool keeps me warm. I click my boots in brackets.
Up here, no one knows it's me. Here! I wave at you.

Keeping the scarf on my brow requires pins and pins.
My poles stab the snow. This feels harder than it looks.

A push angles me downhill. I slalom. *Salaam.*
I am Rumi's chick pea escaped from the boiling

City. I match the black diamond slopes in my skirts.
Men can't catch up. They can't read my thoughts out here.

The Alborz Range muffles my complaints in white blur.
What waits below snow lines, one could almost forget.

Glasses of rose petal tea warm my hands again.
Scent of heated arguments thaws to haunt me.

I suck ice into my lungs to numb them again.
Above, I am a breathless winter sportswoman.

Down there, I am just a woman, one with errands,
A useless degree, crying toddlers, and doubt.

PILGRIM LYRIC

As our boat stretched toward coastline at Jaffa,
I smelled mint, fish, and piss. Warm sea water
Splashed my hand on the starboard. I worried.
Riding from ice for some piece of True Cross,

I remembered the Pardoner further north,
With his rabbit-bone relics, forgiveness
Forged, and I wondered if I were just on
Some fool's errand to this hot Promised Land.

Kneeling here in the empty sepulcher,
My destination was a vacant space,
And it does not disappoint. He's not here;
I am. Some angel folds a spent winding sheet.

I see the imprint on it of absence.
Fear not, says the angel. Believe only.
In this atmosphere of wafted incense,
The smell of some Sufi poet's chick peas,
And the scent of my own perspiration

Heavy with myrrh and my genuflection,

I am convinced. I mark *mappamundi*

Exactly here where some have understood.

ACKNOWLEDGMENTS

I am indebted to my writing teachers, including the late Thomas Lux and Jane Cooper, as well as the living Joan Larkin, Allan Gurganus, who made me understand what it is to be a Southern writer, Marilyn Hacker, and Cornelius Eady. Additionally, I am grateful to Ann Fisher-Wirth, who gave me some initial feedback to my first draft of the long poem in this collection, "The Unborn."

I am indebted to those who have read these works and contributed to their polishing. I am indebted to the publications who have given these poems a forum. I am indebted to my husband, who works hard for us.

"Skiing in Iran" and "Subterranean Lyric #1" appeared in *Across the Margins*.
"Liner Notes" appeared in *L'Allure des Mots*.
"Sunburn Cuisine" appeared in *American Poets and Poetry*.
"Patmos Lyric #1" appeared in *Adelaide* in the United States and Portugal.
"Patmos Lyric 2" appeared in *Coldnoon* in India.
"The Recounting of a Polite Occasion" appeared in *Columbia*, receiving the journal's annual prize.
"The Method" appeared in *Crannóg* in Ireland.

"The Unborn" appeared in *Evergreen Review*.

"Wedding Dishes" appeared in *Grasslands Review*, receiving honorable mention in their editorial contest

"Deceit of Musicals" appeared in *Hidden City Quarterly*.

"Palmistry" appeared in *Karamu*.

"The Victorious Christian Couple" appeared in *Kentucky Review*.

"Your First Poem" appeared in *Left Curve*.

"Between the Keys" appeared in *Oberon*.

"The Drunken Monorail" appeared in *Peaky Hide*.

"Tribulation Lyric #3" appeared in *Perilous Adventures* in Australia

"Botticelli After Savanarola" appeared in *Poetry Salzburg* in Austria.

"Welcome Wagon" appeared in *Quarterly Literary Review Singapore* in Singapore.

"Tribulation Lyric #7" appeared in *St. Petersburg Review*.

"The Astronaut's Wife" and "Microsoft Company Portrait 1978 – and Prophesy" appeared in *Second Nature*.

"The Shark and the Bodyguard appeared in *Slant*.

"Screen Play" appeared in *Sow's Ear Poetry Journal*.

"After the Great Speech" appeared in *Tuck Magazine*.

"At That Time in the City" appeared in *Zaaban* in Pakistan.

About the Author

Anne Babson's first collection *The White Trash Pantheon* won the Colby H. Kullman prize from the Southern Writers Southern Writing Conference in Oxford, Mississippi. She wrote the libretto for the opera *Lotus Lives*, which has been performed in multiple cities and is slated for production once more in Montreal in 2018. She is the author of three chapbooks– *Poems Under Surveillance* is still in print with Finishing Line Press, and she has a forthcoming chapbook from Dancing Girl Press entitled *Dolly Shot*. She has been anthologized in the United States and in England, most recently in the notable collection *Nasty Women Poets: an Unapologetic Anthology of Subversive Verse* released in 2017. Her work has appeared in literary journals on five continents and has won numerous editorial awards. She has been nominated for the Pushcart Prize four times. She has received residency grants from Yaddo and Vermont Studio Center. Her blog about moving south, *The Carpetbaggers Journal*, has close to 50,000 hits and has been picked up by *Y'all Politics* and PBS-related websites. She writes lyrics for a variety of musical projects, most recently a blues album. She teaches writing and literature at Southeastern

Louisiana University. She writes and lives in New Orleans. She will read there at this year's Tennessee Williams Festival.

www.ingramcontent.com/pod-product-compliance
Lightning Source LLC
Chambersburg PA
CBHW071737080526
44588CB00013B/2060